D1371215

NEW YORK

Photographs by Bernd Obermann
Text by Michael Streck

teNeues

There are times when one could wish that the good Lord would start all over again with the Creation and straighten out a few things that didn't turn out so well the first time. He would not have to look long and hard.— He would choose New York City, because everything is assembled there just like on Noah's ark: all cultures, all races, and all religions. The good Lord would probably have a ball in "Babylon on the Hudson", for it is not only the buildings and skyscrapers, the towers and the parks that give New York its face—it is the people. The United Nations are located on the Hudson River, and that is perfectly logical. But in fact, one can see the united nations at any time in the subway, where the world's peoples are united on a space of 430 square feet. It is the people that make New York City more colorful than the brightest ligths on Times Square. New York is rich—and at the same time incredibly poor. New York is both filthy and clean. New York is at the same time decadent an decent, beautiful and ugly. That's not even contradictory. The city is like a human being with all its emotions and moods, full of joy and sorrow.

That is the true charm of New York City.

The New Yorkers say with pride that New York is not America. And fortunately, it is not. New York is a special concept of life and a perpetual experiment. That is why people came and still come into this city, where taxi drivers speak sixty languages and where a subway ride turns into a miniature voyage around the world.

Terrorists have blasted a giant hole in the city, and perhaps New York will never recover from that. To be sure, the hole will be filled up, and trees will grow and buildings arise on the new ground. But the hole is deeper—it is a wound that hurts. The pain will always be part of it. And when cultural critics caustically remark that New York City is cynical, cold, and inhuman, they are at once arrogant and wrong. New York City is the most humane city on this planet—with all the attendant merits and shortcomings.

Michael Streck

Manchmal wünschte man sich, der liebe Gott würde noch mal von vorne beginnen und ein paar Dinge begradigen, die beim ersten Versuch nicht so richtig hingehauen haben. Der liebe Gott müsste nicht lange suchen. Er würde New York wählen, weil dort alles versammelt ist wie auf der Arche: sämtliche Kulturen, sämtliche Rassen, alle Religionen. Der liebe Gott würde sich bestimmt prima amüsieren in Babylon am Hudson. Es sind nämlich nicht die Bauwerke und Wolkenkratzer und Türme und Parks, die New York prägen. Es sind die Menschen. Die Vereinten Nationen haben ihren Sitz am East River, und das ist zwingend logisch. Aber die Vereinten Nationen sind in Wahrheit permanent zu besichtigen in jedem U-Bahn-Wagen. Auf 40 Quadratmetern versammelt sich die Weltgemeinschaft. Die Menschen machen New York City bunter als die schrillsten Lichter am Times Square. New York ist reich. Und unglaublich arm. New York ist schmutzig und rein. New York ist dekadent und dezent, schön und hässlich zugleich. Das ist nicht mal ein Widerspruch. Die Stadt verhält sich wie ein Mensch – mit allen Variationen von Gefühl und Laune, Freude und Schmerz.

Das ist der wahre Reiz von New York City.

New York, sagen die New Yorker nicht ohne Stolz, ist nicht Amerika. Glücklicherweise nicht. New York ist ein Lebensentwurf und ein ständiges Experiment. Deshalb kamen und kommen die Leute in diese Stadt, in der die Taxifahrer 60 Sprachen sprechen und die U-Bahnfahrten kleine Welt-reisen sind.

Terroristen haben ein riesiges Loch in die Stadt gesprengt, und vielleicht wird sich New York City nie davon erholen. Gewiss, das Loch wird zuge-schüttet und Bäume werden darüber wachsen und Gebäude. Aber das Loch ist tiefer und eine Wunde, die schmerzt. Dieser Schmerz gehört nun für immer dazu. Und wenn Kulturkritiker ätzen, New York City sei zynisch und kalt und unmenschlich, dann ist das überheblich und auch falsch. New York City ist die menschlichste Stadt auf diesem Planeten. Mit allen Vor- und allen Nachteilen.

Michael Streck

Il y a des jours où l'on souhaiterait que le bon Dieu recommence à zéro et reprenne ce qui, dans ses créations, n'a pas vraiment été une réussite dès le départ. Le bon Dieu n'aurait pas besoin de chercher longtemps. Il choisirait New York parce que tout y est représenté, comme sur l'Arche de Noé : toutes les cultures, toutes les races, et toutes les religions. Le bon Dieu, à coup sûr, ne s'ennuierait pas à Babylone sur l'Hudson. Car ce ne sont pas les bâtiments ni les gratte-ciel, ni les tours ou les parcs qui font la particularité de New York. Ce sont les hommes. Le siège des Nations unies est situé sur l'East River, et il n'y a là rien de plus logique. Mais en vérité, les nations unies, on les rencontre à tout instant dans n'importe quelle rame du métro new-yorkais. La communauté mondiale se trouve réunie, là, sur quarante mètres carré. Les hommes font de New York une ville de toutes les couleurs, bien plus chatoyantes que les lumières les plus audacieuses de Times Square. New York, c'est la richesse. Et une incroyable pauvreté. New York, c'est la saleté, et la propreté. New York, c'est tout à la fois la décadence et la retenue, la beauté et la laideur. Et ce n'est même pas une contradiction. La ville se comporte comme un être humain, avec tout ce qu'il a de sentiments et d'humeurs, de joies et de douleurs.

C'est cela, le vrai charme de New York.

New York, comme le disent les New-Yorkais non sans une pointe de fierté, ce n'est pas les Etats-Unis. Heureusement que non. New York est le choix d'une certaine forme de vie, et une expérience perpétuelle. C'est pour cela que des hommes sont venus et continuent de venir dans cette ville où les chauffeurs de taxi parlent 60 langues et les trajets en métro sont de vrais petits voyages autour du monde.

Des terroristes ont laissé un trou énorme dans la ville, et peut-être New York ne s'en remettra-t-elle jamais. Certes, le trou sera remblayé et il y poussera des arbres et on y reconstruira des bâtiments. Mais le trou est très profond, il est une blessure douloureuse. Cette douleur fera à jamais partie du reste. Et lorsque des critiques attaquent New York en affirmant que la ville est cynique, froide et inhumaine, c'est arrogant et faux, tout simplement. New York est la ville la plus humaine de la planète. Avec tous ses avantages et tous ses inconvénients.

Michael Streck

Uno desearía algunas veces que Dios empezase todo de nuevo y corrigiese algunas cosillas que en Su primer intento no le han salido del todo bien. Dios no debería buscar durante mucho tiempo. Él elegiría Nueva York porque allí se encuentra de todo como en el Arca: todas las culturas, todas las razas y todas las religiones. Dios se divertiría muchísimo en la Babilonia a las orillas del Hudson. No son los edificios, ni los rascacielos o torres, ni los parques los que caracterizan a Nueva York. Su carácter se lo dan sus seres humanos. Las Naciones Unidas tienen su ubicación en el East River como bien se sabe. Pero la unión de las naciones puede ser observada permanentemente en cualquier vagón del Metro. En esta superficie de 40 m^2 se reúne la comunidad de las naciones. Los seres humanos hacen de Nueva York algo más colorido que las luces del Times Square. Nueva York es rica. E increíblemente pobre. Nueva York es sucia y limpia. Nueva York es decadente y decente, bella y horrible al mismo tiempo. No es siquiera una contradicción. La ciudad se comporta como un ser humano, con todas sus variaciones de sentimientos y humores, alegría y dolor.

Este es el verdadero encanto de Nueva York.

Los neoyorquinos dicen sin ocultar su orgullo que Nueva York no es USA. Por suerte no es así. Nueva York es una manera de vivir y un constante experimento. Por esta razón vino y viene la gente a esta ciudad donde los taxistas hablan más de 60 idiomas y los viajes en Metro son vueltas al mundo en miniatura.

Los terroristas han abierto una gran herida en la ciudad. Tal vez la ciudad no se reponga nunca de esto. Por cierto que la herida cerrará y nuevos árboles y edificios ocuparán su lugar. Pero la herida es profunda y duele. Este dolor será para siempre. Y cuando los críticos manifiestan que Nueva York es cínica, fría e inhumana, sólo son arrogantes o no están diciendo la verdad. Nueva York es la ciudad más humana de este planeta. Con todas sus ventajas y desventajas.

Michael Streck

A volte ci si augurerebbe davvero che Dio ricominciasse da capo e correggesse un paio di cosette che al primo tentativo non ha indovinato del tutto. Non dovrebbe certo cercarle a lungo: gli basterebbe scegliere New York, dove si incontrano tutte le culture, razze e religioni, come sull' Arca di Noè. Dio si divertirebbe da matti nella Babilonia sull' Hudson. Perché non sono gli edifici e i grattacieli, le torri e i parchi che contraddistinguono New York. Sono gli uomini. Le Nazioni Unite hanno la sede sull' East River e questo è assolutamente logico, ma in realtà si possono visitare permanentemente in ogni vagone della metropolitana. Su quaranta metri quadrati si raduna tutta la società umana. Le persone rendono New York più colorata di quanto non lo facciano le luci più variopinte della Times Square. New York è ricca e incredibilmente povera. New York è sporca e pulita. New York è insieme decadente e discreta, meravigliosa e orribile. E non è nemmeno una contraddizione. Questa città si comporta come una persona, ha sentimenti, cambi di umore, prova gioia e dolore.

Questo è il vero fascino di New York.

New York, dicono i newyorkesi non senza orgoglio, non è l'America. Per fortuna. New York è un abbozzo di vita e un esperimento continuo. Perciò si continua a venire in questa città, dove i tassisti parlano sessanta lingue diverse e una corsa in metropolitana è come un piccolo viaggio attorno al mondo.

Il terrorismo ha lacerato la città, che forse non si riprenderà più da questo trauma. Certo, la voragine verrà riempita e si pianteranno alberi e si costruiranno nuovi edifici, ma lo squarcio è profondo, è una ferita dolorosa. Il dolore non smetterà mai. E quello che scrivono caustici i critici saccenti, che New York è fredda e inumana, è arrogante e falso. New York è la più umana tra tutte le città di questo pianeta. Con tutti i suoi vantaggi e i suoi svantaggi.

Michael Streck

BANANA REPUBLIC
BANANAREPUBLIC.COM

ST. PAUL'S
HOUSE
Rev. J. J. D. HALL MEMORIAL
Christ Lives · Trust Him

Table des matières   Directory   Verzeichnis   Directorio   Indice delle materie

Front cover: Madison Square Park, Flatiron Building
Back cover: Subway

Photographs © 2002 Bernd Obermann
© 2002 teNeues Verlag GmbH + Co. KG, Kempen
All rights reserved.

Bernd Obermann
Washington Jefferson Hotel
318 West 51st Street
New York, N.Y. 10019
USA
Phone: 001-212-246-7550
Fax: 001-212-246-7622
Mobile: 001-917-715-7813

Picture and text rights reserved for all countries.
No part of this publication may be reproduced in
any manner whatsoever. All rights reserved.

Photographs by Bernd Obermann, New York
Design by Robert Kuhlendahl, teNeues Verlag
Introduction by Michael Streck, New York
Translation by AMS · Hermann Scharnagl
Horst M. Langer (English)
Florence Marguier (French)
Caterina Polito (Italian)
Eduardo C. Galimany (Spanish)
Editorial coordination by Sabine Würfel, teNeues Verlag
Color separation by O/R/T/, Krefeld, Germany

While we strive for utmost precision in every detail,
we cannot be held responsible for any inaccuracies,
neither for any subsequent loss or damage arising.

Die Deutsche Bibliothek – CIP-Einheitsaufnahme
Ein Titeldatensatz für diese Publikation ist bei der
Deutschen Bibliothek erhältlich.

ISBN 3-8238-4518-7

Printed in Italy

Published by teNeues Publishing Group

teNeues Book Division
Neuer Zollhof 1
40221 Düsseldorf
Germany
Phone: 00 49-(0) 2 11-99 45 97-0
Fax: 00 49-(0) 2 11-99 45 97-40
e-mail: books@teneues.de
Press department: arehn@teneues.de
Phone: 00 49-(0) 21 52-916-202

teNeues Publishing Company
16 West 22nd Street
New York, N.Y. 10010
USA
Phone: 001-212-627-9090
Fax: 001-212-627-9511

teNeues Publishing UK Ltd.
Aldwych House
71/91 Aldwych
London WC2B 4HN
Great Britain
Phone: 0044-1892-837-171
Fax: 0044-1892-837-272

teNeues France S.A.R.L.
140, rue de la Croix Nivert
75015 Paris
France
Phone: 00 33-1-55 76 62 05
Fax: 00 33-1-55 76 64 19

www.teneues.com

teNeues Publishing Group
Kempen
Düsseldorf
London
New York
Paris

teNeues